Joseph Pennell

The Stream of Pleasure

A Narrative of a Journey on the Thames From Oxford to London

Joseph Pennell

The Stream of Pleasure
A Narrative of a Journey on the Thames From Oxford to London

ISBN/EAN: 9783744788502

Printed in Europe, USA, Canada, Australia, Japan

Cover: Foto ©Andreas Hilbeck / pixelio.de

More available books at **www.hansebooks.com**

The STREAM of PLEA-SVRE. A NARRATIVE OF A JOVRNEY ON THE THAMES FROM OXFORD TO LONDON. By JOSEPH AND ELIZABETH ROBINS PENNELL, *together with a Practical Chapter by* J. G. LEGGE

NEW YORK : MACMILLAN & CO.
1891.

THE STREAM OF PLEASURE.

I.

IT was pouring in torrents, on the morning of the 1st of August, when we drove from "The Mitre" down to Salter's boat-house at the appointed hour. Our boat, which was brand new and had not yet been launched, was not ready, and Salter's men seemed surprised to see us. This showed that the weather was even worse than we thought it, and the outlook more hopeless. And yet, during the couple of hours we waited on the rain-soaked raft, two or three other pleasure parties started out in open boats. The girls in the stern, wrapped in mackintoshes and huddled under umbrellas, and the men at the sculls, their soaked flannels clinging to them, looked so miserably wet that we felt for the first time how very superior our boat was.

It was only a pair-oared skiff, shorter and broader than those generally seen on the Thames—"a family boat," an old river man called it with contempt; but then it had a green waterproof canvas cover which stretched over three iron hoops and converted it for all practical purposes into a small, a very small, house-boat. By a complicated arrangement of strings the canvas could be so rolled up and fastened on top as—theoretically—not to interfere with our view of the river banks on bright days; or it could be let down to cover the entire boat from stern to bow—an umbrella by day, a hotel by night.

Under it we could camp out without the bother of pitching a tent. We had already talked a great deal about the beautiful nights upon the river, when we should go to bed with the swans and rise up with the larks, and cook our breakfast under the willows, and wash our dishes and ourselves in quiet clear pools. What if river inns were as extortionate and crowded as they are said to be? we should have our own hotel with us wherever we went. In the midst of a weak and damp hurrah from one ancient boatman, and under a heavy baptism

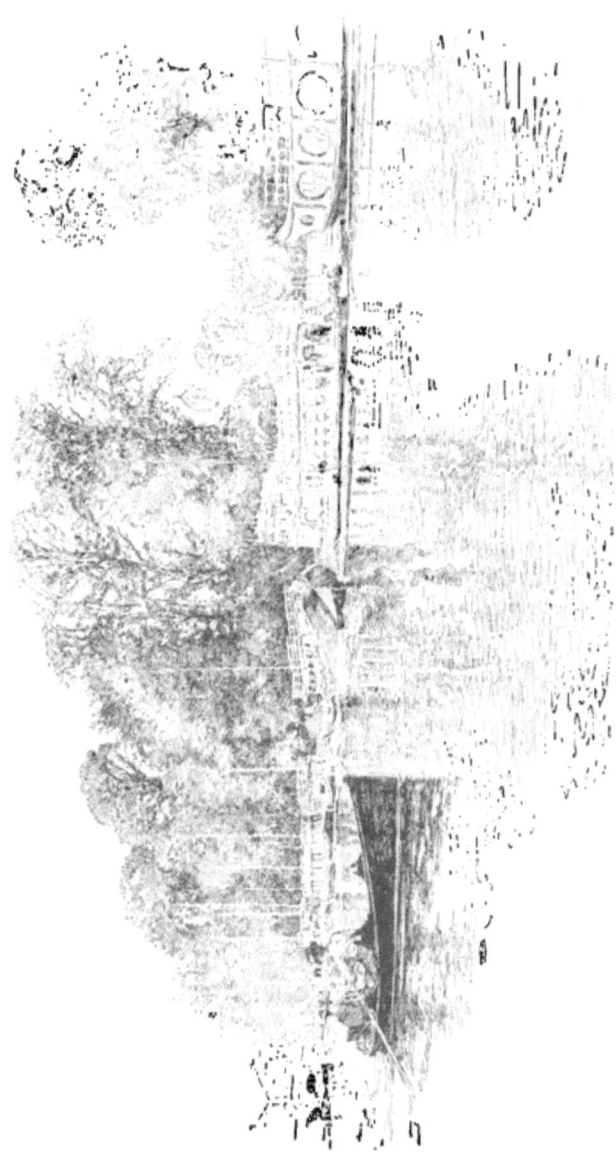

not of champagne, but of rain, the *Rover* was at last pushed off her trestles and with one vigorous shove sent clean across the Thames to the raft where we stood under umbrellas, while Salter's men at once began to load her with kitchen and bedroom furniture. They provided us with an ingenious stove with kettles and frying-pans fitting into each other like the pieces of a Chinese puzzle, a lantern, cups and saucers and plates, knives and forks and spoons, a can of alcohol, and, for crowning comfort, a mattress large enough for a double bedstead. It filled the boat from stern to bow, covering the seats, burying the sculls and boat hooks, bulging out through and over the rowlocks. It was clear if it went we must stay, and so we said, as if we rather liked the prospect of roughing it, that we could manage just as well and be just as comfortable if we slept on our rugs; for we carried all the Roman blankets and steamer rugs we possessed, together with a lot of less decorative blankets borrowed from our landlady in London, and the bundle they made took up the place of two people in the boat. The locker was stored with our supply of sardines, jam, chocolate, tea, sugar, biscuits, towels, and tea-cloths. Our bags were stowed away with the kitchen things. And then at last we crawled into the long green tunnel.

Some one gave us a push. If Salter was looking on from his window, he probably regretted his bargain and wished he had given us the shabbiest old up-river tub in his collection. For in mid-stream the aggressively new *Rover* came to a dead stop, and swung round with the wind. I had never steered, J—— had scarcely ever rowed a boat, and between us we had not the least idea how to manage it. We thought there was a laugh on shore, but we could not see the men who were watching us, as the canvas shut us in on all sides leaving but small loop holes at bow and stern; we were sure we heard some one saying:

"If you're going down the Thames in that boat, you'd better use the right sculls!"

Luckily the river was almost deserted; even the ferry punt had stopped its journeys to and fro, and there was only one small racing boat coming up against the current. Tom Brown says there is space for three boats to pass just here. But it seemed to me there was not too much room for one, and to give the racing man a wide berth, I sent our boat up the Cherwell, where, through the small loop-hole at the bow, I had one charming glimpse of Magdalen tower over the meadows. I do not know exactly how we got back to the other side of the river, but when we found ourselves close to the shores in front of the yellow Isis Inn, we made believe we had come there on purpose, and J——— in a business-like way put back the canvas a little, and got out his sketch block. From here we could again see—I could just manage it by lying down full length and peeping out of the opening at the stern—the far-famed tower, beautiful even in the greyness.

Safe under our shelter, we could enjoy all the beauty of the grey day—the richness of the masses of wet foliage, the softness of the distant trees and fields under their veil of rain, the swaying of the tall poplars in the wind; while the patter patter of the rain on our canvas roof made an accompaniment to the low roar of the near lasher and the rippling of the water against the boat.

I should have been willing to stay there for the rest of the day. I was nervous about our first lock. The river was high after long-continued rains, and for two people who knew nothing about boats and could not swim, the Thames journey with such a stream running was not promising. Already we could hear the noise of the water tumbling over the dam. Then we could see the strong current of the mill race sweeping in a swift-rushing funnel, ready to carry us with it. It looked dangerous, and indeed it is, if you get caught in it. Only the day before, a poor little boy had been drowned here. Now, we were glad to find the lock gates open, so that there was no occasion to hang on to the muddy banks. J—— put his sculls in deep, giving strong but uncertain digs, and pulled them out with a jerk, mindful of Mr. Bouncer's counsel: I cannot call his frantic efforts of those first days sculling. But the lock-keeper, as in the time of Tom Brown, was equal to the occasion. He came out, smoking his pipe with enviable indifference, seized our bow with his long boat-hook, and pulled us into the lock. The great upper gates were slowly closed, he opened the lower sluices, and the water began to fall. At this point, we had been warned, comes one of the dangers of the river journey. For if you lose control of your boat, it drifts across the lock, as happened to Tom Brown on his memorable first row on the river. And even if you keep it close to the side of the lock, if bow or stern catch on the slippery beams or posts found in some locks, especially in old ones, the water, rising or falling, turns you over at once. In fact, it is remarkably easy to upset in a lock, and as difficult to get out again. But then there is absolutely no necessity to upset, and that we were not drowned shows that with ordinary common sense and a little bit of prudence all danger can be avoided.

While the water ran out, the lock-keeper came and gave us that curious literary production, a Thames Lock Ticket. It admits you "through, by, or over the lock or weir" for threepence. That is, I suppose, you can go through the lock in Christian fashion, drown under the weir, push and pull over the roller if there is one, or drag your boat round by the shore; but whether you come out dead or alive, for any of these privileges the Thames Conservancy will have its threepence.

The minute you get through Iffley Lock, you see to its left Iffley Mill. It is only a very old white-washed, brown-roofed mill, with a few poplars, and water falling white below the weir; but the composition is the loveliest you will find between Oxford and London. Every one knows it; it has been photographed, and drawn, and word-painted, until it is as associated with the name of Oxford as is Magdalen Tower or Folly Bridge, and there is no show-place that comes so honestly by its reputation. We were glad we had walked the day before to the little Norman church on the hillside, for now it was too wet to take a step on land. But dry under our cover, we spent two or three hours drawn up, first among the reeds by the tow path, and then under the willows of the island opposite, while J—— worked and I read "Thyrsis" and "Taunt," and exhausted our entire library. On the other side of the lock were three dripping tents, half a dozen wretched men sitting just inside their doors, and at this melancholy sight we vowed that, unless every inn on the river was crowded, we would not sleep out that night.

In the late afternoon we paddled down the quiet stretch between Iffley and Sandford. At Rose Island a dreary boy waited disconsolately with his boat-hook. Further on, a still drearier man in flannels and an eye-glass went by in a canoe, skirting the shore safe out of our reach. Nothing could be prettier than the Thames about here, even in the rain, and it is as simple as Daubigny's Oise. Trees in long straight lines cross the flat meadowland, the river winds lazily between low reedy banks, and large families of ducks come out for a swim where willows bend low into the stream. But this I really discovered the next morning. While we were working our way down to Sandford, I was too much taken up with J——'s entreaties not to send him over the lasher, to think of anything  else. Remembering Tom Brown, I did my best to leave all the river between it and our boat. We found that a lasher, which we had never quite understood, is merely a place above the lock where the overflow of water falls to a lower level, but a place not to be trifled with, as the monument at Sandford reminds all who need the reminder.

Sandford itself, from the river, consists of an old church, a long, low, gabled inn, a big barn, a mill and a lock. When the delightfully picturesque inn came out of the rain, we determined to stay in it even before we knew how bright and fresh it was inside.

Our first day out, we made just three miles!

Into the village we did not go. For one moment, as we finished our tea, the sun showed itself as if in promise of better things. But no sooner had J———— started off with his camp stool, than it went under the clouds again, and the rain fell, and the only change was the gradual deepening of the greyness into night.

The inn was as deserted as the river. Never did a journey begin more uneventfully. The rain had spoiled her season, the landlady told us; no one had stayed with her for a month; and we wondered if we should have to pay to make up for all who had kept away.

II.

THE unexpected is always happening in English weather. We woke in the morning to find the sun shining in through the little leaded windows of our low-ceilinged room, and with the sun came the boats. They kept passing through the lock long before we were off for the day.

And as for our bill, it was so moderate, we made up our minds then and there that camping out was a mistake. Many of the river-side inns are expensive, it is true; you could camp for one-third the price. But then the inns are as comfortable as tents are uncomfortable, and you do not have to do your own household work. It is very pretty to talk about washing dishes in quiet pools, but when you come to try it, it is another matter—a very greasy, disagreeable matter! Probably in a good season inns are so crowded that it is an advantage to be independent of them. But during that very rainy August, comparatively few people were on the upper reaches of the Thames, and crowded hotels never forced us to sleep under odious damp canvas.

Everything added to the cheerfulness of our second morning on the river. Getting through Sandford Lock seemed easy now our green cover was reefed up by its many strings. And if afterwards it hung between the hoops in tantalizing folds, and made an ugly blot in the scenery, it served me as an excellent excuse for the eccentricities of my steering. The shores that were so grey yesterday were now full of colour. Once the long stretch of mud banks was passed, purple flowers fell with the long grass, to the very river's edge; the fields were starred with white and yellow blossoms; clumps of forget-me-nots were half hidden in the reeds, and water lilies floated by. Every tree had a sort of glory round it, and seemed cut out of the landscape, and yet all was suffused with that soft shrouding mist you see nowhere but in England.

I hardly know how long it took us to get to Nuneham. The whole morning we loafed by the bank while

great barges, with gaudily painted sterns, were trailed by slow horses against the current, and men for pleasure towed their skiffs, lifting the rope high above our green top; the sailing boats hurried before the wind, and camping parties, with tents piled high in the stern, sculled swiftly past. As we drifted on, the flat pastures gave way to woods, and by and by we came to Nuncham, the place of the Harcourts, better known the world over as the picnicing ground for Oxford parties during Commemoration Week. There is a very ugly house which fortunately only shows for a minute, and a beautiful wooded hill which grows on you as you wind with the river towards it, and get nearer and nearer, until you reach the pretty cottages at its foot. It happened to be Thursday, visitors' day, and pink dresses and white flannels filled the woods with colour. We moored our boat to the banks opposite the little cottages where a peacock was standing in one of the windows, his tail spread out to best advantage against the thatch, and when two swans floated up and grouped themselves at our side for the benefit of a photographer setting up his camera by our boat, we felt very much as if we were a picture in "Taunt." A big steam-boat, out of all proportion to the river, with a barge in tow, landed a crowd of picnicers on the bridge. The Oxford parties object to these common trespassers upon their preserves; but when men and women on the Thames wear light flannels and pretty dresses it makes little difference, so

far as we are concerned, whether they come from Oxford or from the outer world of common men. They are just as picturesque to look at. We even watched with undisturbed equanimity the two or three steam launches that puffed by, rocking us on their waves, while we did our best to bury or sink the remains of our luncheon. I am proud to say our bottles never floated, but were sent to the bottom for the benefit of future archæologists and antiquaries.

All the afternoon we again drifted with the stream, or lay for hours among the reeds by the banks, watching the boats. In the stillness we could hear the splashing of oars, the grinding of rowlocks long before they came in sight, far voices, and even the sharpening of a scythe on shore. And then a shrill whistle and a train rushing across the meadow-land would remind us that this great quiet of the Thames is within easy reach of the roar of London.

The afternoon, however, ended in a way that was exciting enough. Not long after Abingdon spire showed itself in the flat landscape, we pulled into Abingdon Lock, where there is a fall of several feet. Beyond the lock, the channel is narrow and, owing to the deep fall, the stream is swift. It carried us quickly on until, all at once, as we watched the growth of the spire and the lovely arrangement of the town on the quaint old bridge, we were startled by the shouts of men on both banks. We looked up to see what was the matter, when crash, we went, broadside on, against a stone wall, just here jutting out into the river and dividing it suddenly into two rapid streams, which pass out of sight under the low arches of the bridge. It was well our boat was a broad-beamed family tub; this was the only thing that saved us. The men on the banks, who had been rushing about with boat-hooks and life-preservers, looked immensely surprised when, instead of diving into the water after us, all they had to do was to seize the boat and hold on hard, so as to keep it from rebounding with the blow. It was a ticklish business, and the worst of it was we had been swept up to the wrong pier, and had to trust ourselves again to the current, and come up with another bang at the raft of the Nag's Head Hotel, where the proprietor and a boy, armed with boat-hooks, anxiously waited our violent arrival.

As there is absolutely nothing about this strong current in the many guide books and maps and charts of the

Thames, we could not have been prepared for what is unquestionably one of the few really dangerous places on the river.

Even if we had wished, we could not have thought of sleeping in our boat, when the proprietor of the "Nag's Head" seemed certain he had saved us from a watery grave, and literally dragged us into his inn. We had nothing to regret. We left the boat for another very old and rambling house, another good little dinner. Instead of being alone, as at Sandford, men in flannels were in the coffee room, at the bar, and in the garden. Every time we looked out on the river from the inn windows or from the bridge, we saw a passing pleasure boat.

III.

IN a fault-finding mood, one might complain because there is too much in Abingdon to be seen comfortably during the course of a journey down the river. It is the most picturesque little town on the Thames, as lovely when you look at it from your boat, with its beautiful spire rising above the houses, and its old, rambling flower-grown bridge, the red-roofed " Nag's Head " and garden in the middle ; as when you wander through its gabled streets, coming out now upon the market-place and its town hall by Inigo Jones, now upon the ruins of the old abbey, survival of the day when blood flowed in streams through the streets of Abingdon, and when, darkness covering the land, a red light from a burning monastery, was seen from far up and down the valley of the Thames.

St. Helen's Church is the centre of the town's beauty as of its charity. On three sides the churchyard is

shut in by alms-houses, less famous but no less lovely than those of Bray. I shall never forget this little peaceful corner as we saw it early in the morning. We heard a bell ring, and then down the old timbered cloister of the oldest of the three almshouses, grey-haired, gowned pensioners tottered to prayers in their tiny hall, with the oak panelling on the walls, and the portraits of patrons and benefactors above. And while we lingered, we watched them come out again, gossiping as they came, stopping to look at the flowers that bloomed around the graves, and then passing into the little cloistered rooms, or else up the stairs and along the balustraded *loggia* of the newer brick building. The third is entirely distinct from these, and of another date, with a gable we should call colonial, were it at home, overlooking a little garden

which is as full of gravestones as of flowers. There is a larger garden at the back of the cloistered rooms, where little windows open out on a wilderness of cabbages and peas and onions and gooseberry bushes, with here and there a tall stalk of lilies or cluster of roses, or else a low pear-tree laden with fruit. One or two weedy paths lead through the wilderness, and we saw old men in battered silk hats hobbling down between their crops. Above, from the high-pitched roof, rose the row of tall chimneys, and over all was the sweet smell of many flowers.

Narrow streams, canals with great deep locks opening

into wide basins, and the river Ock wander all around the outskirts of the town, and across them little foot-bridges join the streets to the country roads.

It was not till very late in the day after our arrival that we were ready to leave Abingdon. Then our first care was to stow away the three hoops and the green cover at the bottom of our boat. Our next was to find out something about the current from the landlord. He told us there was no use of our attempting to go down the back way, and we were nervous about again passing, and this time rounding the stone wall. It was in anything but a pleasant frame of mind that we started, the landlord looking after us with evident uneasiness. J—— pulled slowly, apparently with tremendous effort, up above the island, which we cleared so successfully that we ran into the opposite mud bank. Here we made believe, as we always did when we landed unexpectedly, that we had stopped to look at the view and J—— to smoke a pipe. As we pulled off again there came a moment of breathless suspense, and then the boat began to gather headway. The current here was so strong that earlier in the day it had taken all the available loafers of the town to pull a steam tug up-stream against it. Now it caught us, and the first thing we knew we were on the other side of the bridge. It was only here at Abingdon we met with even the suggestion of an accident, so that in the simple tale of our voyage no one need look for Haggardian descriptions of shipwreck.

After the bridge it was easy going. By the time we

had passed Culham Lock we began to take heart again, and actually braved the current of a mill-race in order to explore a little back-water. For one of the great charms of the Thames is the number of these " sedged tributaries," which wander far from the main stream through green pastures and between lines of willows and sweet flower hedges. Often their entrance is so overgrown with reeds and lilies you can scarcely find it, and the boats that pass beyond are few in number. Sometimes the back-water flows to or from a mill, sometimes it is really the main river which is left by the boats for the cut to the lock. But the most beautiful are those which seem to tire of running with the current, and turn from it to rest where lilies blow round long islands, or where cattle graze in quiet meadows.

As we worked slowly in and out of the willows, a man on shore glanced at us so hard, we knew he must own the water. And sure enough, as soon as we were within hearing, "This is private water," he yelled.

"Oh, thank you!" said J——, politely, "we shall know another time!" When you are master of the situation you can afford to be polite.

Of course the man who is proprietor of a river bank, and fancies the water also is his property, looks upon all boating parties as trespassers. River travellers are apt to look upon him as a nuisance, and to tell him so, following the advice of the well-known R. A. The wonder is the entire Thames from London to Oxford is not placarded Private!

We landed, while the enemy still glared, and walked

the short distance to Sutton Courtney, for of the beauty and freedom from tourists of this little village one great

river authority has written much. We would not advise any one to go out of their way to visit it; its old cottages are in good order for the visitor who is supposed never to come.

As the swift mill-stream carried us back to the river, we did our best to bring down a picturesque old stone bridge, dashing up against it in fine spirited style. But our boat was staunch; it seemed, these first days, to know it must take care of itself and of us into the bargain.

It was near Clifton Lock, we first saw Wittenham Clump, the hill with a group of trees on top, which is after this, for many miles, for ever cropping up in the most unexpected places, now before you, now behind, giving a good idea of the many windings of the river. We had come, too, into the region of tall clipped elms, which from here to London are one of the most beautiful, if familiar, features of the Thames.

IV.

THERE was no sleeping in the boat that night, for we had appointed a friend or two—the Publisher and the Parson—to meet us at the thatched house, known as the "Barley Mow," which stands on the high road on the other side of the river from Clifton Hampden. River men often make it their resting-place and taste a cup of ale there, for which liquor, as well as for substantial lunches and teas and dinners, and queer little bedrooms hidden away under the thatch, the house is very remarkable. For this there is the testimony of many in the Visitors' Book, among others

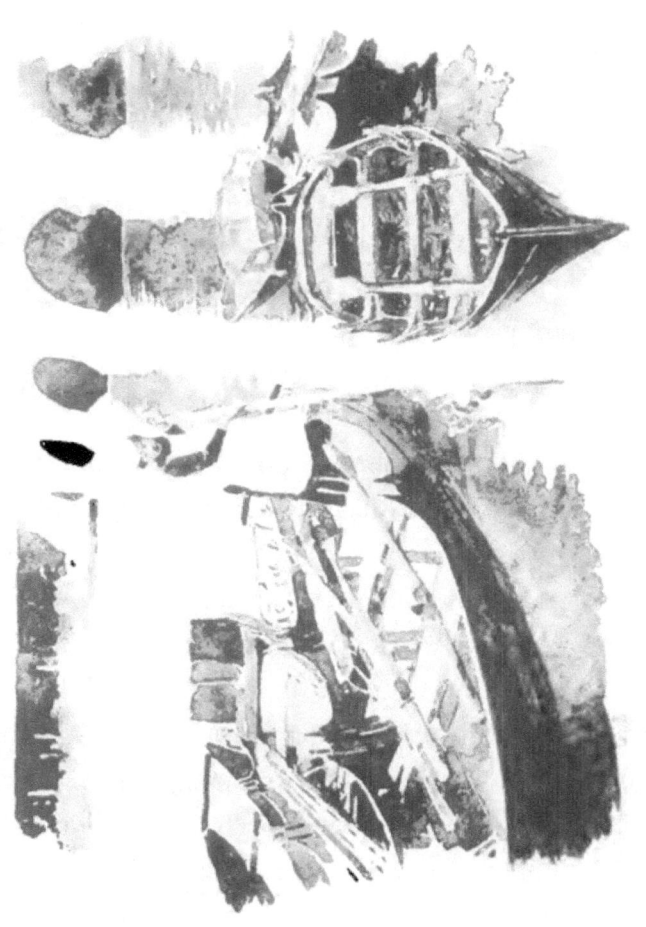

of the Lazy Minstrel, and if he be not an authority on the Thames, then no man is. The hostess is always, with talk running fast as the river, waiting upon hungry people, in the little parlour, where one window looks out on the high road, and the other on the garden, in August full of tall poppies run to seed, and the walls are panelled, and the ceiling is so low every new-comer knocks his head against its huge beam.

We got to Clifton Hampden on Friday evening; all day long on Saturday there was a constant going and coming. We never went out on the road between the inn and the river that we did not meet a stream of men in flannels and bright blazers; women in blue serges, gay blouses and sailor hats, on their way to the "Barley Mow." We never went to the landing-place that we did not see launches and skiffs and punts (and once the *Minnehaha* and the *Hiawatha*, two real canoes) either passing by or pulling to the shore where the pretty girl was ready with her boat-hook. It was strange how even the record-breakers, at other landing-places in such a hurry to be off, found time to stop and help her, or to watch her as she skilfully punted her way in and out of the great mass of boats, put some under the bridge for the night, brought out others for the crews about to start.

Here all was life and movement, while Clifton Hampden itself, where the thatched cottages are scattered along the elm-shaded road, and climb to the church high above the river, seemed to sleep peacefully day and night. Only the schoolhouse, with its large clock-face and loud bell, gave signs of life. If you went into the Post Office, where sour balls and ink-bottles were the chief stock-in-trade, you started a little bell jingling as you opened the door; but

it was five minutes or more before the postmaster came in from the near fields, bringing the smell of hay with him. Fishermen slumbered on the river banks, and there was always one punt, stationed almost under the shadow of the little church, in which on three chairs sat three solemn men who never stirred, except when one, still holding fast to his line with his left hand, with his right lifted up a great brown jug, drank long and deep, and handed it to the next, and so it passed to the third. The sun shone, the rain fell, the shadows grew longer and longer and the jug lighter and lighter, but whenever I passed, there they still sat.

By evening so many people had come to the " Barley

Mow" that a dozen or more had to be quartered in the village. The Publisher and Parson were put in a delightful little cottage, with roses clustering at its door. But we, having come first, were given the best chamber—the Honeymoon Room, the landlady called it; and all that afternoon she had kept showing it to the boating parties who had lunched or taken tea with her. " The lady won't mind," I would hear her say as she opened the door. But evidently the visitors did, for if I looked up it was only to see tall figures in white flannel beating a hasty retreat among the poppies.

When candles were lighted and pipes brought out in the little panelled parlour, the profane Parson gave us the legend of the place, and thereat the Publisher and a wicked Barrister made unseemly sport. For he said that once Ruskin, as he stood here by the river with the light of sunset falling upon it, and watched the flaming and fading of the pools among the rushes, and the water hurrying from under the brick arches, saw a little boy run from one side of the bridge to the other, and lean far over the parapet with eyes fixed upon the current beneath. Of what was he thinking, this little boy? Was it of the hurry of the water, of the beauty of the evening, or had this speed and loveliness already awakened him to higher and holier thoughts? And as Ruskin wondered, a boat drifted from under the arches into the light, and the little boy, leaning still lower, spat upon the oarsmen, and dodged quickly and ran away, and Ruskin went home a sadder, if a wiser, man.

All the elm-lined roads and willowed backwaters near the "Barley Mow" lead to pretty villages; to Long Wittenham, which deserves its adjective, with its one street straggling far on either side its old cross; to Little Wittenham, as worthy of its name, but a group of tiny houses with a no less tiny church and lime-scented churchyard just at the foot of Wittenham Clump; and to Dorchester, with its huge abbey church, perhaps best worth a visit. But the great beauty of Clifton Hampden and the neighbouring villages will not let itself be told; and he will never know it who does not feel the charm of peaceful country when the sunset burns into the water and the elms are black against the glory of the west, and little thatched cottages disappear into the darkness of the foliage—the charm of long walks through hedged-in lanes as the red fades into the gray twilight, and a lone nightingale sings from the hedge, and far church bells ring softly across the sleeping meadows.

We devoted Sunday to the visit to Dorchester, so as to

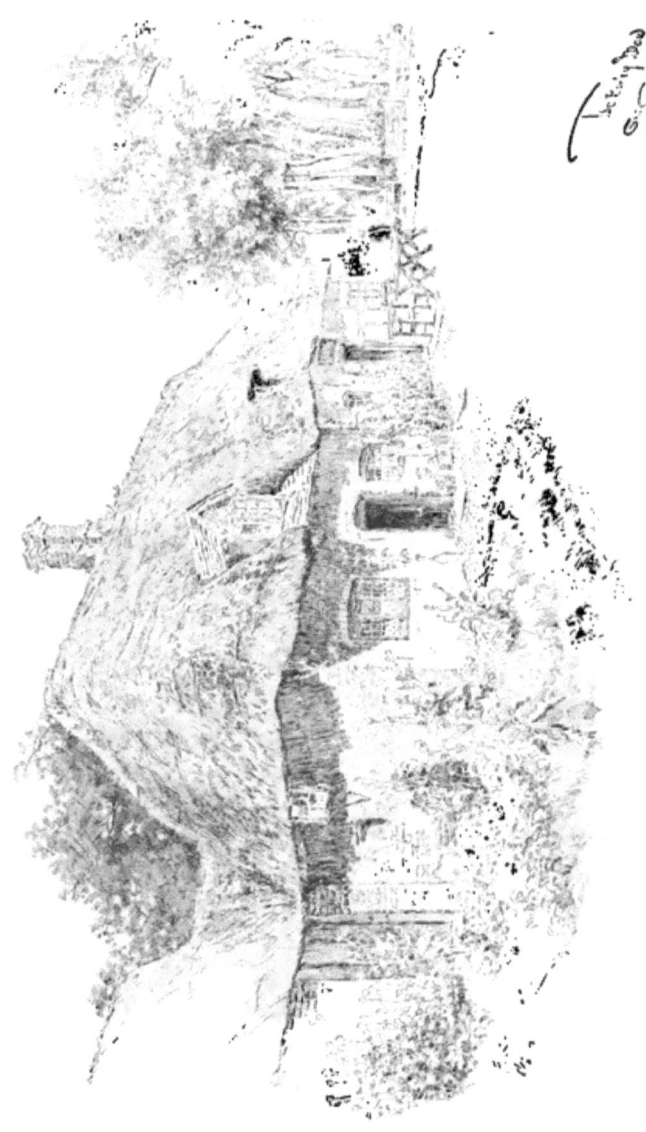

explore the little river Thame, which runs into the Thames so modestly and quietly, you might, were you not on the look-out, pass it by unnoticed, though, according to the poets, it is the bridegroom who here meets and weds the fair Isis on her way from the Cotswolds, and thus joining, they form the Thamesis, and together flow on, through London town, into the sea. In the quiet little village to which the Thame leads was once the cathedral church of the great kingdom of the West, already established in the days of the Venerable Bede. The church, rebuilt and altered and restored, still stands, bare but beautiful, and in Dorchester to-day are not enough people to fill it, even were it without rivals. But close by is the little chapel with cross on top, the rector of which, rumour has it,—and this is the strangest fact of modern Dorchester—is the author of the *New Antigone;* and while we were in the town a large detachment of the Salvation Army beat their drums through the quiet streets. Long after the boatman, a genuine Cap'en Cuttle, had pushed us away with his hook, and we were winding with the Thame between the pollards, their rude music came to us over the wide pasture land.

We turned homeward towards Clifton Hampden just at the

hour when kettles were boiling in every boat. On the river every one makes afternoon tea, just as every one wears flannels ; and so, of course, we felt we must make it with the rest. We pulled up a little backwater and landed with our stove among the willows. The Publisher went to the near lock for water, the Parson filled the spirit lamp. The trouble was great and the tea was bad, and I mention the incident solely because this was the only time during our month on the river that the stove was disturbed. From that time forward it rested from its labours in the box in which Salter had packed it, and for the privilege of carrying it with us we afterwards paid in our bill.

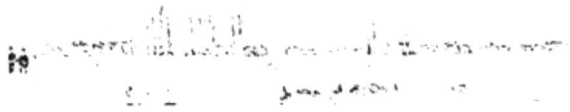

V.

WE left the "Barley Mow" on Monday morning under a grey, threatening sky. But it was Bank Holiday, and not even the occasional showers could keep the boats at home. Many went by decked with water lilies; tents on shore were gay with flags. Those river fiends, the steam launches, were out in full force, puffing past and tossing us on their waves, and washing the banks on either side. We began to think that after all it is rather aggravating to see the angler aroused from contemplation, the camper interrupted in his dish washing, the idler disturbed in his drifting, and sometimes the artist and his easel upset, all for people who turn their backs on the beauty of the river and play "nap" and drink beer or champagne, as they might in the nearest public-house or club at home.

The great business of the day with everybody, however, was eating and drinking. The thin blue smoke of camp fires rose above the reeds. In small boats kettles sang and hampers were unpacked. In the launches the cloth was never removed. And in these narrow upper reaches, we could look across the river into camps and boats and see what every man was eating for his dinner.

After Shillingford, where the arches of the bridge framed in the river beyond, and its low island, and the far blue hills, and where, near "The Swan," 'Arry and 'Arriet were romping, Benson, a few red roofs straggling landward from a grey, pinnacled church tower, came in sight, and to Benson we walked for lunch. The village is at its best seen from a distance; its church is restored into stupidity; its inns, survivals of coaching days, are less picturesque than their associations.

Our resting-place for the night was Wallingford, a town with much history and little to show for it. When we pulled ashore it was raining hard, and we went at once to the old gabled "George," where we found a German street band and a great crowd, and horses trotting through the courtyard, and occasionally trying to make their way into the Coffee Room. It was the day of the Galloway Races, whatever they may be, and local excitement ran high.

The band kept on playing while we ate our tea in company with a party of flannelled record-breakers who were in fine spirits. They blew their own trumpets almost as loud as the cornets outside because they had sculled twenty miles since morning. "Not bad for a first day out, by Jove, you know!"

"Twenty miles," said J——, not in the least impressed; "why, we may have come only eight by the map, but it was full twenty and a half by the Parson's steering."

Later, when the landlady came in for orders, they called for beer for breakfast, but we asked for jam. "Jam by all means," said J——; "we're training to make our four miles a day," which was our average. After this they would have nothing to do with us, but drank whisky and wrote letters at one end of the table, while at the other we studied the visitors' book, and learned how many distinguished people, including our polite critic Mr. William Black, had been at the "George" before us.

VI.

NEXT morning the Parson and the Publisher took an early train for London, and we were again a crew of two. It is impossible to be the first boat out in the morning; early as we thought we were, other travellers had started before us. Already, while we loaded our boat, campers were sculling swiftly past and under the bridge, and punts were leisurely hugging the opposite shore.

The punt is to the Thames what the gondola is to the canals of Venice. But a few years ago Mr. Leslie regretted it was not more popular on the upper river. Now, wherever you go, you see the long straight boat with its passengers luxuriously outstretched on the cushions in the stern, the punter walking from the bow and pushing on his long pole. To enjoy his work he must know not only the eddies and currents of the stream, but something of the river bed as well. For this reason it is not easy to punt in unknown waters. Countless as were the punts we saw, I do not remember one laden as if for a trip. The heaviest freight was a dog, a baby, or a lunch-basket. As often as not a girl was poling, and I never ceased wondering how work, that looked so easy, could be as difficult to learn as punters declare it. But these are the three situations, I am told, which the beginner at the pole must brave and conquer before he can hope for ease and grace: first, that in which he abandons the pole and remains helpless in the punt; secondly, that in which, for reasons he will afterwards explain, he leaves the punt and clings to the inextricable pole; and thirdly, that of fearful suspense when he has not yet decided whether to cling to the pole or the punt.

By the shores beyond Wallingford, here and there houseboats were moored. The typical Thames house-boat is so big and clumsy, with such a retinue of smaller boats, sometimes even with a kitchen attached, that it is not so easily moved as the big hotels we used to see wandering on wheels through the streets of Atlantic City. Indeed, because of the trouble of moving, it often remains stationary summer after summer. One we caught in the very act of being poled down stream; another we saw just after it had finished an enterprising journey; the rest looked as if nothing would tempt them from their moorings. They do not add much picturesqueness to the river. A square wooden box set on a scow is not and can not be made a thing of beauty. At Henley Regatta when the flat top becomes gay with flowers and Japanese umbrellas and prettily dressed women, colour makes up in a measure for ugliness of form. But on many house-boats we passed that day from Wallingford, buckets and brooms and life-preservers were the only visible ornaments.

As if defiant in their bareness, they were drawn up in the least lovely corners of a river on which you must go out of your way to escape loveliness. One was just by a railway bridge in full view of every passing train; others were close to shadeless shores where the afternoon sun poured hot and scorching on their thin wooden walls.

The inns, by the way, were a pleasant contrast. Nothing could be prettier than the little Beetle and Wedge, red and gabled, with a big landing-place almost at the front door; or the Swan at Streatley, with its tiny lawn where the afternoon tea-table was set, as in every other riverside garden we had passed above and below Cleve Lock.

It would have been foolish indeed to put up for the night under our canvas when in Streatley a whole cottage was at our disposal, once we could find it. We rang up the postmistress, whose door was shut while she drank tea like the

rest of the world. She directed us to a little brick cottage with jasmine over the door where lived a Mrs. Tidbury; and Mrs. Tidbury, armed with a key big enough to open all Streatley, led the way almost to the top of the hilly road, to a cottage with deep thatched roof and a gable where an angel, his golden wings outstretched, his hands folded, kept watch. *Nisi Dominus Frustra* was the legend, in brass-headed nails, on the door which opened from the front garden into a low room with great rafters across the ceiling, and a huge fireplace, where every morning of our stay we saw our bacon broiled and our bread toasted. There were

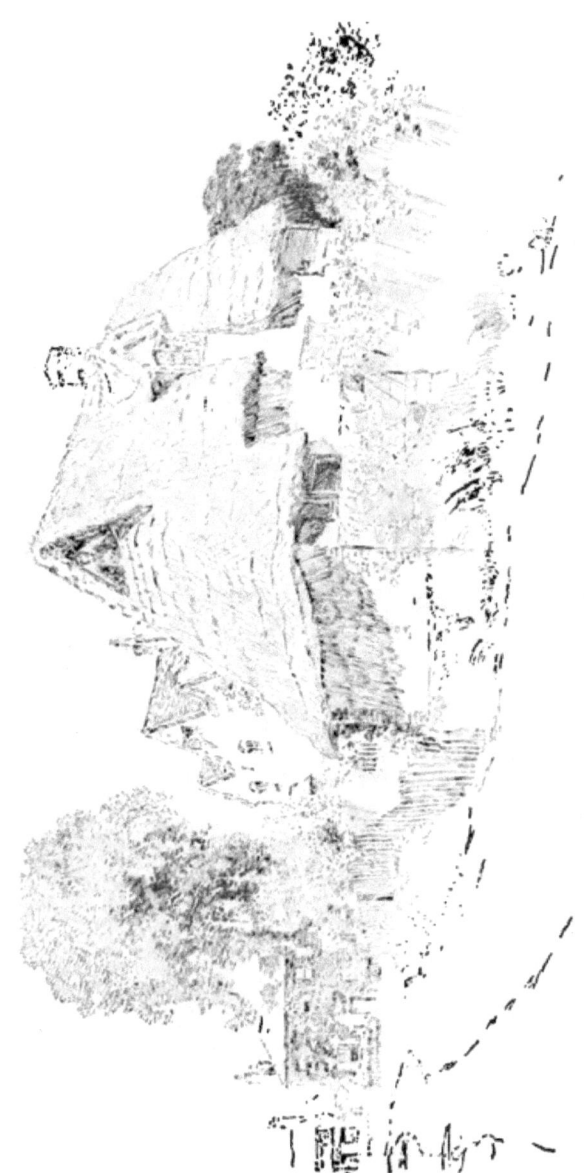

jugs and jars on the carved mantelshelf; volumes of Balzac and Tourgueneff, Walt Whitman and George Eliot, Carlyle and Thackeray, on the book-shelves; photographs from Florentine pictures on the walls; brass pots hanging from the rafters. A narrow flight of wooden steps led up to a

bedroom with walls sloping under the thatch. Mrs. Tidbury gave the big key into our keeping; in the morning I bought meat from the butcher in Goring, and coaxed a cross old man into selling me green pease and berries from his own garden. We were at home, as we were bidden to be, by the friend whose pleasure it is to share with others those good things which are his worldly portion.

"And Streatley and Goring are worthy of rhyme," sings the Lazy Minstrel, whose lays are the Gospel of the River; and of paint too, according to Mr. Leslie. The pretty

village streets and the old bridge which joins them have been done to death; of Streatley Mill we have had our fill; Goring Church, with the deep red roof and gray Norman tower, so beautiful from the river, is almost as familiar in modern English art as the solitary cavalier once was in

English fiction. The campers, who pitch their tents on the reeded islands, are armed with cameras, and on the decks of house-boats easels are set up. But

> "When you're here, I'm told that you
>   Should mount the Hill and see the view;
> And gaze and wonder, if you'd do
>   Its merits most completely."

It was the hour of sunset when we mounted and looked down on the valley, spread out like a map below, the river winding through it, a path of light between the open fields, a cold, dark shadow under the wooded banks. May the Lazy Minstrel another time wait to smoke and weave his lazy lay until he has climbed the hill, and then he will sing of something besides "The Swan" at Streatley!

VII.

THE day we left Streatley, the hot August sun had come at last. It was warm and close in the village, warm and fresh on the water. The *Golden Grasshopper*, the famous yellow and white houseboat of the last Henley Regatta, had just anchored near "The Swan," and its proprietor was tacking up awnings and renewing his flower frieze, which sadly needed the attention, but he monopolized the energy of the river. Boats lay at rest under the railway bridge below Streatley and under the trees of Hart's Woods.

In riverside gardens children practised what Mr. Ashby-

Sterry calls "hammockuity." Anglers dozed in the sun. The only living creature who seemed awake was a vulgar little boy who, when we passed a sheepwash in a pretty backwater and asked him when the sheep were washed, told us, "Why when it's toime, of coorse."

"O, Pangbourn is pleasant in sweet summer time,"

with its old wooden bridge to Whitchurch over the river, and the lock with delicate birches on its island, and the mill and the weir and the gables and red roofs and tall elms. In all Thames villages the elements of picturesqueness are the same; in each they come together with new beauty.

We had scarce left Pangbourn before we passed Hardwick House, red, gabled, and Elizabethan, and the more impressive because, as a rule, the big private houses on the Thames are ugly. And not far beyond was Mapledurham Mill, a fair rival to Iffley, and Mapledurham Lock, which many people, beside Dick in Mr. Morris' *Utopia*, "think a very pretty place"; and on the other side of the lock Mapledurham House, of whose beauty every one tells you. But you cannot see it from the river, and its owner will not let you land. His shores are barricaded by

the sign "Private"; there is no inn in the village; he has but lately asked the courts to forbid fishermen to throw their lines in the Thames, as it flows past his estate; and the only wonder is that he has not hung up a curtain in front of the beautiful trees that line his river bank.

There is an inn, "The Roebuck," just a little below—a new red house, tiled and gabled, standing on a hill that overlooks the river. But, convenient though it was to the beauties of Mapledurham, we did not care to stop in it; it suggested certain hotels we know on the Wissahickon at home, or on Coney Island.

It was about here, in the cool of the evening, that the anglers awoke. From a punt, where a young lady in big hat and green ribbons, and a man in a blue flannel jacket, sat side by side under the shade by Mapledurham Ferry, we heard a jubilant cry, "O Paul, already!" And Paul drew up his line and a man in a near boat paddled up to see, and on the hook hung a fish no longer than a minnow. And next, an old man, in long black alpaca coat and tall hat, waved his hands towards us and begged our help. He had a bite, and for half an hour had been trying to get his fish out of water.

"A whale!" asked J——.

"No, a young shark," answered another elderly man dancing round the alpaca coat in excitement.

J   with a scull pushed gently under the line, and the old man pulled and pulled and pulled, and at last, up came a bunch of weeds!

From here to Caversham is the stupid stretch of which guide and other books give fair warning. But at the hour of sunset the ugliest country is glorified, and nowhere is the river really ugly. The "Dictionary of the Thames" for 1888 recommended as "snug and unpretentious" the White Hart Inn on the left bank by Caversham Bridge. Accordingly, to the left bank we drew up, but behold! we found a large hotel, a steam launch bringing in its passengers, waiters in dress-coats, a remarkably good supper, and a very attentive Signor Bona to add the pleasure of an Italian kitchen to the clean comfort of the English inn.

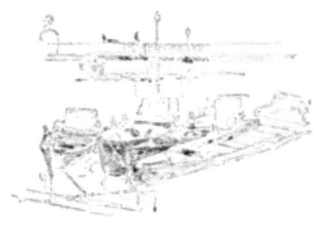

VIII.

THE town of Reading.

> " 'Mong other things so widely known
> For biscuits, seeds, and sauce,"

seldom has a good word said for it by those who write from the river point of view. And yet the stream of the Thames makes glad the city with its railways and big brick factories and tall chimneys, and it becomes, in its own way, as picturesque, though not as characteristic of the upper Thames, as the little villages and the old deserted market towns. It is not, however, the ideal place for a house-boat, and for this reason, I suppose, we found two or three within hearing of the ever-passing trains and within sight of the chimneys and the smoke. From them, canoes were carrying young men and their luggage to the convenient station; in the small boats at their bows young ladies were

lounging; in the sterns white-capped maids were busy with brooms and buckets.

Even if the much-abused banks, where the river the "cleere Kennet overtakes," were unattractive, it is not far

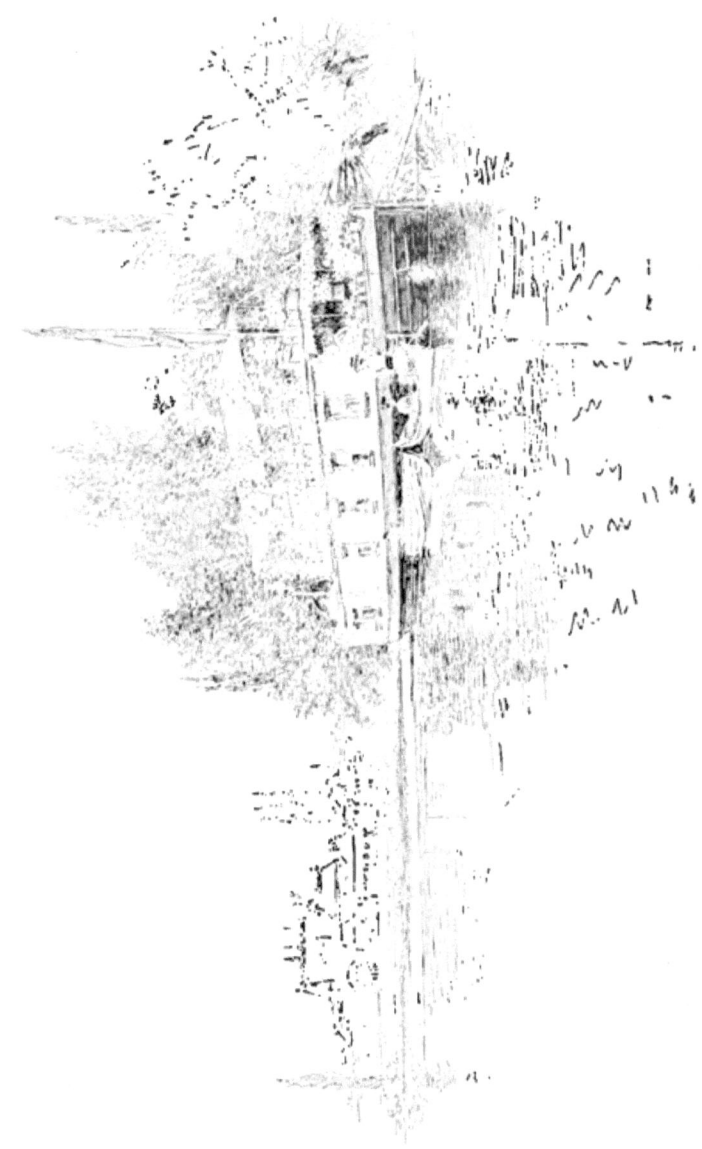

to Holme Park and the shady riverside walk, known as the Thames Parade, beyond which is Sonning Lock,

> "That's famed
> For roses and for bees,"

and for the lock-keeper who cared for them until his death some three years ago, and whose poem called "Summer Recreations" is perhaps the simplest description ever written of the journey from Oxford to Windsor. Close to the lock is the village, "set on fair and commodious ground," with roses and sweet jasmine growing over every cottage door. It was at the cheery "White Hart" the Lazy Minstrel lunched

> "Off cuts of cold beef and a prime Cheddar cheese
> And a tankard of bitter at Sonning."

We too might have had our tankard in its pretty garden, but there was no room for us; and so we walked from the river through the churchyard to "The Bull," low and gabled, running round two sides of a square, with the third shut in by the churchyard wall and a row of limes. It would be a figure of speech, however, to say we stayed at "The Bull," where we ate our meals and paid our bill.

But our rooms were in one of the near cottages; and as for the Publisher, when he drove up in a hansom from Reading Station, he was given a freehold property all to himself.

It was chance that took us to "The Bull." Now we

find from Mr. Black that it was quite the correct place to go. For "The White Hart," down by the riverside, he says, is beloved of cockneys, but the artists who know the Thames swear by "The Bull."

We thought Sonning quite the prettiest village we had come to, and J—— and the Publisher and the Parson thought the barmaid quite the nicest. But, to counterbalance these attractions, the weather was vile. All Sunday drenching mist fell. Books are the last things to be looked for in riverside inns; boating men have something better to do than to read. In only one did we find

anything in the shape of literature in the coffee-room; and there, a volume of *Meditations on Death and Eternity* had been left for the delectation of people very busy with life and the present. In many of the inns there was not even a newspaper to be had. If there was one, as at Sonning, it was sure to be the *Daily Telegraph*, just then full of the

"Is Marriage a Failure?" question. But somehow time did not hang very heavy. As we stood at the door we heard the famous church bells, which a century ago carried off a two-handled silver cup for the "superior style in which they rang ten hundred and eight bob-major," and for this we would much sooner have the word of the guide-book than hear for ourselves the way really beautiful bells can be misused in England. We sat in the church porch and listened to the hymns of the congregation. We walked to the bridge where men and women watched for clear weather, while on the near island campers pathetically huddled together under the trees. But just in the hour before dark, the mist rose and the clouds rolled away to give fair promise for the morrow.

A gale was blowing, but no rain fell when we pulled—for to-day there was no easy drifting—to Wargrave. The poplars looked cold and bare, the willows showed all their silver, and at Shiplake Lock, as J—— and the Parson to the best of their ability gave the familiar Thames cry of "Lock! Lock!" and we waited for the gates to open, the wind swung our boat clear round, and it took a deal of manœuvring with the boathook to bring the bow in position again. A young man from a near tent ran up to play lock-keeper—the favourite amusement of campers in the intervals between eating and cooking—and hardly had we passed through when—a certain proof of the beauty of

Wargrave—we suddenly saw Mr. Alfred Parsons sailing home from his work to "The George and Dragon."

Wargrave bears an air of propriety, as befits the last resting-place of the creator of "Sandford and Merton." Carriages with liveried footmen roll by on the village street, upon which new Queen Anne houses open their doors. The artistic respectability of "The George and Dragon" is vouched for by its painted sign, the not very wonderful work of two R.A's. On each side the inn, lawns slope down from private houses, and boats lie moored along the shore. And, as if to show they are not common folk, the boating men of Wargrave go so far as to make themselves ugly and wear a little soldier cap stuck on one side of their heads.

But little of the time we gave to Wargrave was spent in the village. We explored instead, the

"Loddon slow, with verdant alders crowned,"

and the many near back-waters, with that indifference to the sign "Private water" which Mr. Leslie in "Our River" recommends. Indeed, no one seems to heed it. I have heard men read aloud " Private water," and add at once, "Oh, that's all right. Come on!" In Patrick Stream, as the only man who ever really painted English landscape told us, there are Corots at every step, and what more need we say? In Bolney back-water the trees meet above your head, and in the water below, with here and there a glimpse beyond the willows of lovely poplars and

old farmhouses and "wide meadows which the sunshine fills." Reeds and lilies and long trailing water plants in places choke the stream, so that sculls are put away for the paddle. May and sweetbrier, with the bloom all gone now

in mid-August, trail over the banks. Flowering blackberries festoon the bridges, where you must lie low as you float under the arch. The stillness is broken only by the plashing of your paddle and the twittering of birds; the dragon-fly comes to dream on the water, blue kingfishers fly from shore to shore, and the water-rat swims across the track of your boat. The solitude is seldom disturbed, except perhaps by a boy in a dinghy, by the one-armed ferryman of Wargrave in a punt coaching a beginner, or by a canoe silently stealing along.

In the quiet of the evening it was pleasant to pull back to "The George and Dragon" in time to see the sun sink, a ball of fire, below the wide stretch of golden meadowland opposite, where villagers played cricket after their day's work.

From Wargrave, past the colony of house-boats within easy distance of Shiplake Station, at the foot of a shady lane, where, if you land, a man suddenly appears and claims a penny (for what I hardly know); past Bolney with its ugly big house and pretty islands where the swans rest at noontide ; past the ferry where the Lazy Minstrel sat and sang "Hey down derry!" until the young lady came to his rescue; past Park Place with its grotesque boat-house, niched and statued; through Marsh Lock, at whose gates during Regatta week boats crowd and push and jostle, just as people do at the pit doors of a popular theatre:—'tis a short three-miles' journey to "The Angel" at Henley.

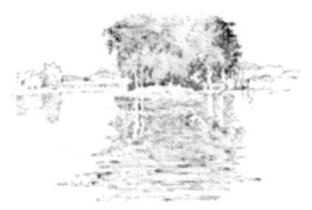

IX.

HENLEY seemed quiet by comparison with the July day when we came down from London and found the river a mass of boats and brilliant colours, and the banks crowded with people, and Gargantuan lunches spread at "The Lion" and "The Angel" and "The Catherine Wheel." But that was during Regatta week, when Englishmen masquerade in gay attire and Englishwomen become "symphonies in frills and lace," and together picnic in house-boats, launches, rowboats, canoes, punts, dinghies, and every kind of boat

invented by man. It is true that now and then the course is cleared and a race rowed :

> "But if you find a luncheon nigh
> A mayonnaise, a toothsome pie
> You'll soon forget about the race."

But whatever life there was at Henley we saw from "The Angel." Across the way was the "finely toned, picturesque, sunshiny Lion," where Shenstone wrote his famous lines, too often quoted to be quoted again, and where the coach starts for Windsor. The pretty bow-window of our coffee-room opened upon the river, and grey as were the three days, we waited in vain to see Henley in sunshine, pleasure parties were always starting from the landing-place, boats never stopped passing, swans floated by in threes, while boys forever hung over the open balustrade of the old grey bridge, where, now and then, we could see the long boats on Salter's van as it crept Oxford-ward. It is this bridge which is adorned with the heads of Isis and Thamesis, whose praise by Sir Horace Walpole was a piece of family log-rolling one hundred years or more before the expression was invented.

A strong wind was blowing and there was quite a sea on

when, late one afternoon, we pulled away from "The

Angel," under the bridge, down the Regatta reach, wide

and desolate without its July crowds ; by the island with its little classic temple and its poplars set against a background of low hills—the starting-point of the race ; past many houses, among others that of Mr. W. H. Smith, an improvement on the usual Thames-side house ; and then, like the "countless Thames toilers, now coming, now going," we took our pink ticket at Hambledon Lock, where there is a red lock-house covered with creepers, close to a great weir, and a mill-stream, a white mill, and a little village full of yellow gables and big deserted barns, with grass growing on their old roofs and weeds choking their neglected yards.

We landed just below the lock, determined to break a record. For I fancy never before has any one on the Thames journey succeeded in making but nine miles in a week! We put up at a brand-new, very ugly, but comfortable brick "Flower Pot," where there was a landlord who had much to say about art and the Royal Academy. For Royal Academicians often lunch with him, and Royal Academy pictures have been painted under the very shadow of his house, as well they might, for all the near country was as pretty as the inn was ugly. Elms, the loveliest in the whole length and breadth of England, met overhead in the narrow lanes, bordered the fields "with poppies all on fire," and shut in the old-fashioned gardens full of weary sunflowers waiting to count the steps of the sun that would not shine. Here and there through the

elms we caught a glimpse of the river, and in the distance the tower of Medmenham Abbey.

We dropped down to the Abbey towards noon the next day, just as the first picnic party was landing in the near meadows. For this place, where for centuries men worked in silence and knew not pleasure; where later those who wore the brown robes obeyed no law but the *Fay ce que l'oudras* carved above their doorway, is now but a popular picnicing ground. Even in its degeneracy, however, it is true to its traditions. Medmenham monks, of the Cistercian order and of the Hell-Fire Club, were alike in this: whatsoever their hands found to do, they did with their might; they were no less great in vice than in virtue. And so to-day, those who come there, picnic with all their might, and are great in the lunches they spread upon the grass and the games of tennis they play on the lawn of the big new hotel, where we saw a Gentleman Gipsy's van in the shade and a Gentleman Waterman's boat by the shore. We, too, have lunched at Medmenham. We had been but a few weeks in England then, and I remember how we wondered at the energy of the young girls in fresh muslins who unpacked the hampers, laid the cloth, and washed the dishes; and how we thought nothing could be prettier than the old Abbey turned into a farmhouse, with its cloisters and ivy-grown ruined tower. That was four years ago, and in the interval we have seen much of England's loveliness. Now, we were not so much impressed, though the Abbey makes a pleasant enough picture, with its grey ivied arches and red roof and tall chimneys, and the beautiful trees on either side. Even the tower, if it be but a sham ruin, is effective. The *Fay ce que l'oudras* of the

eighteenth-century Children of Light can still be read above the old door, and he who would know how differently men can interpret the golden rule of the Monks of Thelema has but to turn from Besant and Rice's well-known novel to the less famous hundred years' old story of *Chrysal*.

At Lady Place, but little more than a mile below, men came together to save their country from the Stuarts. But in a boat under a blue sky, drifting past hay-scented meadows, sightseeing loses its charm, and it was a relief to be told by the lock-keeper that some of the family were now at home and so the gates of Lady Place were closed against the public. There was nothing to see anyway; just a few tablets stuck in the walls, and a cellar where a conspiracy went on once—he couldn't exactly say just when.

"O, Bisham banks are fresh and fair"; and Bisham Abbey stands where it cannot be hid from the river, and you need not leave your boat to see the old grey walls and gables or the weather-worn Norman tower of Bisham Church, past which Shelley so often drifted as he dreamed his dreams of justice. For by Marlow shores, in Bisham Woods,

> "Or where, with sound like many voices sweet,
> Waterfalls leap among wild islands green,"

he, like Lord Lovelace and the knights at Hurley, conspired to set men free.

Great Marlow was a disappointment. Only the street which leads to the river, where the ferry was of old, shows a few picturesque gabled houses. Gravel was heaped on the shores, where the girls stand in Fred Walker's picture, and instead of the ferry-boat, pleasure punts and canoes and skiffs lay beyond. The town was poor in Shelley's time. When he was not seeking to establish a moral world governed by the law of love, Mrs. Shelley tells how he was busy going about from cottage to cottage, seeking to lessen the heart-rending evils of the people among whom he lived, until in the end, he shared part at least of their misery; a severe attack of ophthalmia was the price he paid for his charity.

Now, Marlow, to the outsider, looks fairly well to do. It shares in the prosperity of the river. Launches are for ever bringing pleasure parties to "The Anglers" on the river bank. As we learned to our cost, that very day "The George and Dragon" had provided lunches and dinners and teas for "three fifties." One fifty was disporting itself upon the river to the imminent danger of the red-skirted, white-bodiced girls in canoes and the men in racing boats. When dinner-time came we found that not only the hotel larder, but apparently the town larder also had been emptied.

X.

IF you wake up early enough in "dear old Marlow town" you will see all the men in flannels walking riverward you met yesterday in boats, each with a towel over his arm. They are on their way "to headers take at early dawn." And presently, if it be Sunday morning, after the breakfast hour, the procession reforms and divides, one half in top hats and conspicuous prayer books, the other still in flannels and carrying hampers instead of towels. For Sunday is the river day on the stretch between Marlow and Maidenhead.

When we came downstairs in the morning, an Oxford

friend had just arrived to take a pair of sculls for the day, and it was in fine style we made our start. Dickens in his "Dictionary of the Thames" advises caution in passing Marlow Weir. Though, as a rule, he is as nervous as "Taunt" is easy-going, his nervousness here is not without reason. The weir, less protected than many, stretches to your right as you go towards Marlow Lock, and the angler-haunted current by the mill is on your left and you must keep straight in the middle, or what is the result? You go over, as so many have already gone, and, once over, you never come out again. But still, on the Thames, with moderate care there is no occasion for accidents so long as daylight lasts, for at every weir is the sign "Danger!" big enough to be read long before you come to it. After dark, however, even those who know the river best are not safe.

"And Quarry woods are green"; and at the foot of low hills, yellowing with the late harvest, is Bourne-End, a group of red roofs and a long line of poplars; and next Cookham church tower comes in sight. Under its shadow Fred Walker lies buried near the river he loved in life. Within the church a tablet is set up in his honour in the west wall, and a laurel wreath hangs beneath. But over his grave only a grey stone, like those one sees in all English country graveyards, is erected to his memory, and that of his mother and brother.

At the Ferry Hotel at Cookham we unpacked our boat

and ceased to be travellers, to become, with the many on the water, pleasure-seekers of a day. Anglers no longer slept on the banks, but were alert to order us out of their way if we drew too near. In every house-boat, in every steam launch, was a gay party. Along the beautiful stretch between Marlow and Cookham, beneath the steep wooded slopes of Cliefden—where here and there the cedars and beeches leave a space to show the great house of the Duke of Westminster rising far above, its gray façade in fine perspective against the sky—up the near back-waters winding between sedge and willow, one to a mill, another to a row of eel-butts, the name of the smaller boats was

legion. Among them was every possible kind of row-boat, and there were punts, some with one some with two at the pole, dinghies, sail-boats, even a gondola and two sandolas, and canoes with single paddle, canoes with double paddles, and one at least with an entire family on their knees paddling as if from the wilds of America or Africa. On the Thames it seems as if no man were too old, no child too young, to take a paddle, a pole, or a scull. In one boat you find a grey-haired grandfather, in the next a little girl in short frocks and big sun-bonnet.

The locks were more crowded than usual, and on their banks men waited with baskets of fruit and flowers. In one we sunk to the bottom to the music of the " Brav' Général," and the musicians, when there was no escape, let down the lock-keeper's boathook with a bag at the end for pennies.

But it was outside Boulter's Lock, on the way back to Cookham, that we found the greatest crowd. There was such a mass of boats one might have thought all

> " The men who haunt the waters,
>   Broad of breast and brown of hue,
> All of Beauty's youngest daughters,
>   Perched in punt or crank canoe,"

were waiting to pass through together. But presently the lock-keeper called out, " Keep back ! There are a lot of boats coming !" and the lock gates slowly opened and out they came, pell-mell, pushing, paddling, poling, steaming, and there was great scrambling, and bumping, and meeting of friends, and cries of " How are you ? " " Come to dinner at eight," " Look out where you're going !" and brandishing of boathooks, and glaring of eyes, and savage shoutings, and frantic handshakings, and scrunching of boats, and scratching of paint, and somehow we all made our way into the lock as best we could, the lock-keeper helping the slower boats with his long boathook and fitting all in, until there was not space for one to capsize if it would. But indeed in a crowded lock if you cannot manage your own boat some one else will manage it for you; and, for that matter, when there is no crowd you meet men whose only use of a boathook is to dig it into your boat as you are quietly making your way out. Both banks were lined with people looking on, for Boulter's Lock on Sunday afternoon is one of the sights of the Thames.

When the upper gates opened, there was again pushing and scrambling, and it was not until we were out of the long cut and under the Cliefden heights that we could pull with ease. The boats kept passing long after we had got back to Cookham and while we lingered in the hotel garden. Almost the last were the sandolas and the gondola, and as we watched them, with the white figures of the men at the oar outlined against the pale sky and bending in slow, rhythmic motion, we understood why these boats are so much more picturesque than the punt, the action of the gondolier so much finer than that of the punter. The entire figure rises above the boat, and there is no pause in the rhythm of the motion. In a punt the man at the pole, except in the upper reaches near Oxford, stands not above but in the boat; and fine as is his action when he draws the pole from the water and plunges it in again, the interval when he pushes on it or walks with it is

not so graceful. To know the punt at its very best you should see it in a race, when the action of the punter is as continuous as that of the gondolier.

Gradually the launches began to hang out their lights,

the row of house-boats opposite Cookham Church lighted their lamps and Japanese lanterns, making a bright illumination in one corner, and "when the evening mist clothed the riverside with poetry as with a veil," "all sensible people" turned their backs upon it and went in to dinner.

After Cookham, there is history enough to be learned from the guide-book for those who care for it: scandalous as you pass under

> "Cliefden's proud alcove,
> The bower of wanton Shrewsbury and of love;"

stirring about Maidenhead, where the conspiracy of Hurley bore some of its good fruit; mainly ecclesiastical at Bray, where lived the famous Vicar, Simon Aleyn, who never faltered in his faith unless the times required it:

> "Whatsoever king shall reign
> Still I'll be the Vicar of Bray, sir."

He showed his good taste. The village is as charming when you first see from the river the long lines of poplars and the church tower overlooking a row of eel-butts, as when you wander through the streets to the old brick almshouse with the quaintly clipped trees in front and the statue of the founder over the door. For the first time in our river experience there was not a room to be had in the village. At least so the landlady of "The George" on the river bank told us, while she struggled with her h's. She

advised us to try at the H-h-hind's H-h-head in the village. We did, but with no success. Now was the time to unfold our canvas and put up in our own hotel. Instead, we dropped down-stream in search of an inn where we should not have to make our own beds and do our own cooking.

Between Bray and Boveney Locks is the swiftest stream in the river, and we saw only one boat being towed, and another sculled with apparently hard work up past Monkey

Island, where the Duke of Marlborough's painted monkeys, which give the island its name, are said still to climb the walls of his pleasure house.

The river flowed in long reaches and curves between

shores where there was little to note. But as we passed Queen's Island we saw the great grey mass of Windsor Castle gradually coming into view on the horizon. We lost sight of it when, with a turn of the stream, we came to Surly, where the Eton boys end their famous 4th of June, and to little Boveney Church, shut in by a square of trees much as a Normandy farm is enclosed. Just before the lock the castle was again in front of us, nearer now

and more massive. But hardly had we seen it when it went behind the trees. Below the lock dozens of boats and many swans with them were on the water; not the crowd we had left at Maidenhead, however. Men sculled in stiff hats and shirt-sleeves. Parties were being pulled instead of pulling themselves. Soldiers, their little caps still stuck on their heads, but their elegance taken off with their coats, tumbled about in old tubs: once in the midst of them a crew of eight, spick and span as if for a parade and coached by an officer passed in a long racing-boat.

The banks, where fishermen sat, grew higher and more commonplace; one or two little back-waters quietly joined the main stream. A long railway embankment stretched across the plain. The river carried us under a great archway, and just before us, Windsor towered, grand and impressive, from its hill looking down upon river and town. The veil of soft smoke over the roofs at its foot seemed to lift it far above them, a symbol of that gulf fixed between royalty and the people.

Rain began to fall as we drew up to a hotel on the Eton side, just opposite to where the castle "stands on tiptoe to behold the fair and goodly Thames."

In the town we could forget the river, so seldom did we see the river uniform, so often did we meet tourists with red Baedekers. In the hotel we could as easily forget the town, for here we overlooked the water and the passing boats. Even when it was so dark that we could no longer see them, we could hear the whistle of the steam launches, the dipping in time of many sculls, and the cries of coxswains.

XI.

THE morning we left, Windsor was brilliant with sunshine. *Keep well to the right* is painted in big letters on the upper side of the bridge. For facing you as you pass through the middle arch is the sharp point of land familiarly known as the Cobbler, which separates the lock cut from the main stream; and when the river is high the current is strong, and many are the unwary whose boats have been dashed against the Cobbler. But he looked peaceable enough, a punt stationed just in front, as we passed. And now, we could face the strongest current without a doubt.

Near Romney Lock the red walls and grey chapel of Eton came in sight, and when we looked back it was to see a corner of Windsor Castle framed by the trees that line the narrow cut. Beyond the lock were the beautiful Eton playing fields, where crowds meet on the 4th of June; and next Datchet and Datchet Mead, where

Falstaff was thrown for foul clothes into the river; and Windsor Park, where the sun went under the clouds and down came the rain in torrents. At the first drop all the boats disappeared. The minute before, a girl had been poling down-stream at our very side. Now she had gone as mysteriously as the Vanishing Lady. We, not understanding the trick, kept calmly on our way and were none the worse for our wetting. And when the sun shone again the boats all reappeared as suddenly. One cannot tell in words how the river, with the first bit of sunshine, like the Venetian lagoons, becomes filled with life.

At Old Windsor the weir seemed to us much the most dangerous we had come to, and the lock by far the most dilapidated. After we left the lock we passed the yellow bow-windowed "Bells of Ousely," an inn famous I hardly know for what, its sign hanging from one of the wide-branching elms that overshadow it; and Magna Charta Island, where the barons claimed the rights which they have kept all to themselves ever since, and where two or three pleasure parties were picnicing, and a private house stands on the spot so sacred to English liberty; opposite, those who to-day are its defenders were playing at making a pontoon-bridge, and the field was dotted with red coats and white tents. Below, was Runnymede, a broad meadow

at the foot of a beautiful hillside, where the great fight was fought.

At Bell Weir Lock the gates were closed. Too many barges had crowded in from the lower side, and the last had to back out, an operation which took much time and more talk. A boat-load of campers pulled up while we waited. "Back water, Stroke!" cried the man at the bow, who had a glass screwed in one eye. "Easy now! Bring her in! Look out where you're going!" And with his glass fixed upon Stroke, he quite forgot to look out where he was going himself, and bang went the bow into a post and over he tumbled into a heap of tents and bags at the bottom of the boat. When he got up the glass was still there, as it apparently had been for several weeks, for we had seen the party going up-stream when we were at Sonning. They had probably been to the top of the Thames and were on their way back, but they had not yet learned to manage a boat. When the gates at last opened Stroke saw some young ladies on shore, and at once put his pipe in his mouth and his hands into the pockets of his blue and black blazer, and struck an attitude, and Bow gave orders in vain. The boat swung from one side of the lock to the other and still he posed. However, we had the worst of it in coming out. For in trying to clear the waiting barge we ran aground and stuck there ignominiously, while all the boats that had been behind us in the lock went by. But it was not much work to push off again, and almost at once we were in Staines.

The town is thought to be the rival of Reading in ugliness, an eyesore on the Thames. We minded this but little, for we spent the evening sitting at a table in the garden of "The Pack Horse," watching the never-ceasing procession of boats—the punt with the two small boys come to meet their father after his day in London;

the racing punts; the long, black canoe, either the *Minnehaha* or the *Hiawatha* (it was too far away to see its name); the picnic parties coming home with empty hampers; the sail-boats; the ferry punt, where now and then an energetic man in flannels took the pole from the ferryman and sent the punt zig-zagging through the water, but somehow, and in the course of time, always got to the other side. And if an ugly railway bridge crossed the river just here, we could look under it to the still busier ferry, where the punt, crossing every minute, was so crowded with gay dresses and flannels that one might have thought all Staines had been for an outing. The sun set behind the dense trees on the opposite bank, its light shining between their trunks and the dark reflections; moonlight lay on the water, and still we sat there. We could understand our landlord when he told us that, though he had travelled far and wide, there was no place he cared for as he did for Staines. Like his wife and the pile of trunks at the head of the stairs, he had an unmistakable theatrical look. Later he went into the bar and played the violin, and people gathered about the tables while he gave now a Czardas, now the last London Music Hall song. The evening was the liveliest we spent upon the river.

A fine Scotch mist fell the next morning. Of the first part of the day's voyage there was not much to remember but grey banks, a grey river, and an occasional fishing-punt with umbrellas in a row. In our depression we forgot when we passed Laleham that the village has become a place of pilgrimage. Matthew Arnold lies buried in its churchyard, and perhaps he, who hated the parade of death, would rather have the traveller pass his grave without heeding it than stop to drop a sentimental tear.

At Chertsey the mist rose and our spirits with it. We had arrived just in time for the Chertsey Regatta, and when presently the sun struggled through the clouds, as if by magic the river was crowded with boats. The races were not worth seeing. The men sculled in their vests, poled in their suspenders. Punts at the start got so hopelessly entangled that spectators roared with laughter. But there was an attempt to do the thing as at Henley. Between the races, canoes and punts and skiffs went up and down the racecourse, and the people in the two houseboats received their friends and tea was made. Among the lookers-on, at least, costumes were correct.

From the river, Chertsey was so pretty and gay, we

did not go into the town, which Dickens says is dull and quiet, even to hunt for the humble nest where Cowley

> "'Scaped all the toils that life molest,
>   And its superfluous joys,"

or the mansion where Fox raised his turnips.

We neared Shepperton Lock as the sun was going down. Just below, the long straggling village of Weybridge was hidden round a corner of the river at the mouth of the Wey. Close by another little stream and a canal join the Thames, and their waters meet in the weir pool, which was a broad sheet of light when we first saw it. At the landing-place of "The Lincoln Arms" lay the usual mass of boats, but almost all were marked with monograms repeated on every scull and paddle, and on the road above carriages with liveried footmen waited.

The little river Wey runs to Guildford and still farther through the fair county of Surrey, and on its banks, not far from Weybridge, lived the rollicking, frolicking, jolly old monks whose legend is said to drive away sentiment as suddenly as a north wind scatters sea-fog. But after all, if you turned from the Thames to explore every stream rich in story and in beauty, you would never get down to

London. Besides, on the Wey there are locks every hour or less, and at almost all you must be your own lock-keeper and carry your tools with you, and there are those who say the pleasure is not worth the work.

From Weybridge to Walton is the neighbourhood abounding with memories of olden time, where Mr. Leland once went gypsying. There is first Shepperton, with its little Gothic church and many anglers, on your left, and then Halliford, a quaint old street facing the river, where we found the *Shuttlecock* moored to the landing-place. Who but the Lazy Minstrel has a right to row or sail, paddle or pole a *Shuttlecock*  on the waters of the Thames? But an impudent young man we had never seen, came down the steps, boarded her, and paddled away as placidly as if he had nothing to be ashamed of! And next came Cowie Stakes, where Cæsar is said to have crossed the Thames, pulling up ruthlessly the stakes driven in by the Britons— "He is the sort of man," Mr. Jerome says, "we want round the back-waters now." And then Walton, with its relics of days when scolds were called by their right name, when gallantry was the fashion and astrology a profession. For if there is a picture at every turn of the Thames, there is a story as well; and if you are not too lazy, you read it in your guide-book and are much edified thereby, but you go no further to prove it true.

The cut to Sunbury Lock, with its unpollarded willows and deep reflections, was like a bit of a French canal. At the lock there was one of the slides found only in the most crowded parts of the river. On these, boats are pulled up  an inclined plane over rollers, and then let down another into the water above or below, as the case may be, and this in one-fifth of the time it takes to go through a lock, nor is there any long waiting for water to be let out or in.

And after Sunbury came Hampton, where a large barge with red sail furled showed we were nearing London; and close by Garrick's Villa with its Temple of Shakspere; and on the opposite shore Moulsey Hurst, where the costermongers' races are run in the month when gorse is in bloom, and where I was first introduced by the great Rye Leland to Mattie Cooper, the old gipsy, whose name is an authority among scholars. And here the river divides into two streams to run round islands, which stretch one after another almost to Moulsey, so that as you pass down on either side the river seems no wider than it was many miles away at Oxford.

At Moulsey Lock on Saturday afternoon and on Sunday you find everything that goes to make a regatta but the races. It is the headquarters of that carnival on the river which begins with June, is at its height in midsummer, and ends only with October. Not even in the July fêtes on the Grand Canal in Venice is there livelier movement, more graceful grouping or brighter colour. There may be gayer voices and louder laughter, for the English take their pleasure quietly. But I do not believe that men in their every-day amusements can show a more beautiful pageant anywhere. The Venetian fêtes can be seen only once each summer. But though for that of the Thames you must go to Henley Regatta, every week Boulter's or Moulsey Lock makes a no less brilliant picture. And as Mr. Leland has said, " It is very strange to see this tendency of the age to unfold itself in new festival forms, when those who believe that there can never be any poetry or picturing in life but in the past are wailing over the banishing of Maypoles and all English sports."

XII.

IT was still early Saturday afternoon when we reached Moulsey. At once we unloaded our boat and secured a room at the Castle Inn, close to the bridge and opposite that

> " Structure of majestic frame
> Which from the neighbouring Hampton takes its name."

The rest of the day and all the next we gave to the river between Hampton and the Court. In the lock the water never rose nor fell without carrying with it as many boats as could find a place upon its surface. At the slide, where there are two rollers for the boats going up and two for those coming down, there were always parties embarking and disembarking, men in flannels pulling and pushing

canoes and skiffs. Far along the long cut, boats were always waiting for the lock gates to open. And on the gates, and on both banks, and above the slide, sat rows of lookers-on, as if at a play; and the beautiful rich green of the trees, the white and coloured dresses, the really pretty women and the strong, athletic men, casting gay reflections in the water, made a picture ever to be remembered. On the road were ragged men and boys, with ropes and horses, offering to "tow you up to Sunbury, Shepperton, Weybridge, Windsor," and still raggeder children chattering in Romany and turning somersaults for pennies. If we pulled up to Hampton it was to see the broad reach there "overspread with shoals of labouring oars," or with a fleet of sailing boats tacking from side to side—dangerous, it seemed to us, as the much hated steam launches. Below the weir were the anglers' punts. And up the little Mole, which "digs through earth the Thames to win," the luncheon cloth was spread and the tea-kettle sang under the willows. But however far we went, when we came back to the lock, it was only to find the same crowd, to hear the same endless grating of boats over the rollers, the same slow paddling out through the gates, the same fall of the water over the weir, and above all other sounds, the monotonous cries of "Tow you up to Sunbury, Shepperton, Weybridge, Windsor." All the long Sunday afternoon the numbers of boats and people never lessened, though the scene was ever varying. And when the sun sank below Moulsey Hurst, there was still the same crowd

in the lock, there were still the rows of figures sitting on the banks; the men and horses on the road, the stray cycler riding towards Thames Ditton—all now, however, but so many silhouettes cut out against the strong light.

Close to Moulsey Lock is Hampton Court, with its park and gardens, its galleries and courts, its bad pictures and fine tapestries, its fountains and terraces. What good American who has been in England does not love this most beautiful of English palaces? But of all those who come to it Sunday after Sunday, there is scarcely one who knows that within a ten-minutes' walk is another sight no less beautiful in its way—very different, but far more characteristic of the England of to-day.

XIII.

AT Moulsey we felt that our journey had really come to an end; but everybody who does the Thames is sure to go as far as the last lock at Teddington, and so for Teddington we set out early on Monday morning. There is no very fine view of Hampton Court from the river. One little corner, crowned with many twisted and fluted chimney pots, rises almost from the banks, and the wall of the park follows the towpath for a mile or more. On our left we passed Thames Ditton, where, in the Swan Inn, Theodore Hook, who to an abler bard singing of sweet Eden's blissful bowers would " Ditto say

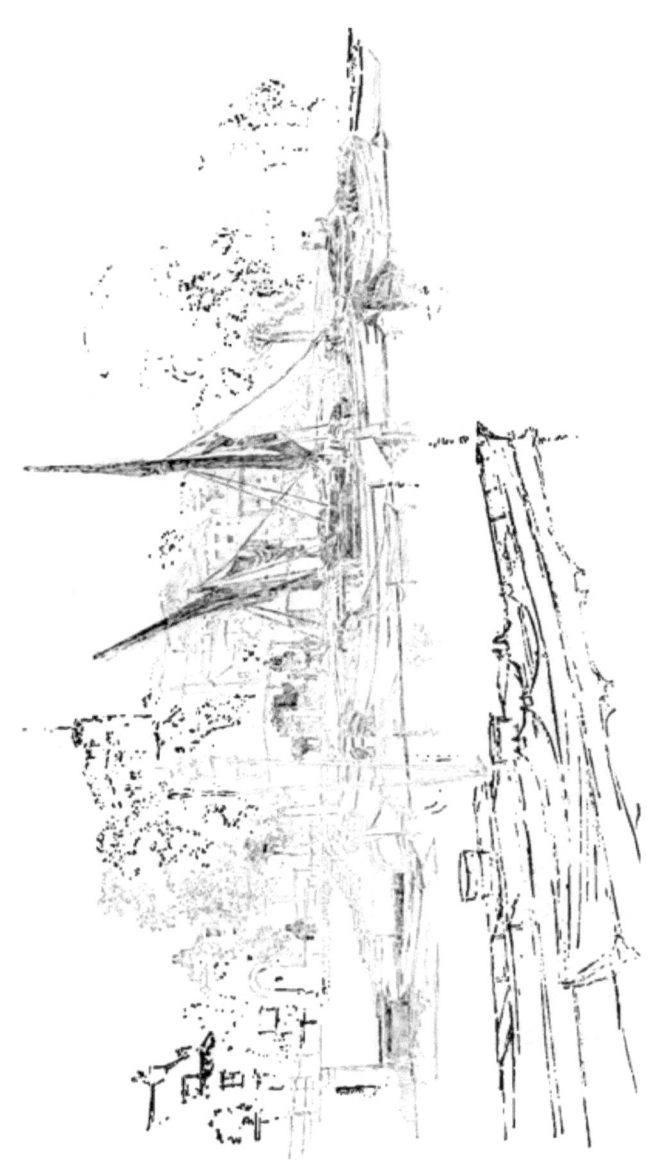

for Ditton," is as often quoted as is Shenstone at "The Lion" at Henley; and Kingston, with its pretty church tower, where the great coal barges of the lower Thames lay by the banks, and a back-water we explored degenerated into a sewer; and then we were at Teddington with its group of tall poplars, where there is a large lock for the barges and steam tugs, and a smaller one and a slide as well for pleasure boats, and where the familiar smoky smell that always lingers over the Thames at Westminster or London Bridge greeted us.

The tide was going out or coming in—it was so low we hardly knew which—and now on each side the river were mud banks. But it was still early, and we decided to pull down and leave our boat at Richmond. After Teddington it was ho! for Twickenham Ferry, and the village of eighteenth-century memories. From the river we saw the villa where Pope patched up his constitution and his grotto, and where to-day the Labouchere family patch together gossip and finance and politics and call it *Truth;* and the mansion where the princes of the house of Orleans lived in banishment; and many other villas and cheerful houses and terraced gardens, with their associations of wits and courtiers, on either side — all this very delightful, as Fitzgerald wrote in one of his letters. And in front of us rose Richmond Hill, where Turner painted and many poets have sung, and "The Star and Garter" overlooked the Thames's "silver winding

way," but not the memory of the "lass" who inspired the sweetest of old English songs or even "to call her mine" on the C in *all*, delayed our steps, for we should be bankrupt if we had stopped.

In places the shores were as pastoral as in the upper narrow reaches, but again we came to the mud banks. From every landing-place men cried, "Keep your boat, sir?"—for Salter has agents on the river whose business it is to take care of boats left by river travellers until his van calls to carry them back to Oxford. Everybody expected us to stop; something of that great noise of London, which has been likened to the loom of Time, seemed to reach us. We had left the Stream of Pleasure and were now on the river that runs through the world of work, as the big barges and the steam tugs told us. At Richmond we pulled up to shore for the last time, and intrusted the *Rover*, with a good deal of its paint scratched off and many honourable scars of long travel and good service, to the waiting boatman, and so

"At length they all to mery London came."

A PRACTICAL CHAPTER.

THE writer of this chapter is really a modest person, and in venturing to give some practical hints on boating on the Thames, he thinks it just as well to state the fact. The chapter is not, however, intended for the members of any Thames rowing, sailing, or canoe club, nor for those sensible Cockneys whose custom it is, summer by summer, to pass a few spare days towing up or drifting down the placid reaches of the river. It is meant for the visitors to London whose knowledge of the Thames is limited to glimpses of it at Westminster and Richmond, or possibly at Windsor and Oxford; and for the indolent Londoner, who knows Hampton Court, perhaps, and the Surbiton Waterworks, but has never smoked a pipe on Streatley Bridge or in the back-water below Cookham Lock. Its object is to show how easily the beauties of which this book has treated may be seen by any one who has energy enough to catch a fairly early train. The Thames is not the least bit coy, and a more innocent siren would be hard to discover. If the sage warnings given earlier in these pages as to weirs and locks be observed, and never more than one person at a time stands upright in the boat, the row from Oxford to London is as free from danger as a walk from Charing Cross to the Bank. And now to business.

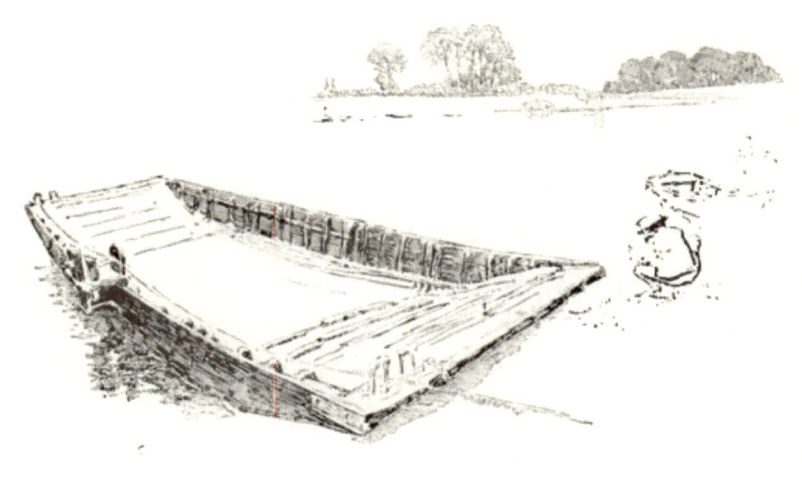

BOATS.

MUCH need not be said on this head. Most watermen will see that you are at least safely boated; and you are not likely, unless you are anxious for it, to be planted in a racing-shell which takes months of practice to sit. One word of advice may be given. Those who know a little, but not enough, about pleasure-boating, are often fascinated by what is known as a half-outrigged boat. For real comfort, however, they are to be sneezed at; the broad-beamed inrigged boat is everything. The more saucer-like the better. As regards oars or sculls, use sculls by all means, if you can. In a broad-beamed boat there is no doubt you will make better way with them, and find them less fatiguing. The advantage of oars is that half-an-hour's practice (in a safe "tub," as comfortable boats are often called) will enable any reasonably athletic man to jog along with enjoyment for half a day.

In most parties there will probably be at least one who can manage sculls; and for a party *the* boat is a randan, propelled by both oars and sculls, with a stern more or less roomy to suit your numbers. The sculler sits on the centre thwart, bow and stroke use oars, and the three of them can easily row down stream seven passengers, or even more.

Towing cannot be recommended, unless there is one of the party who understands it, or unless you set about it very gingerly. Towing appears to one at first sight as simple an operation as driving a perambulator. But a first attempt may be dangerous, and is certainly as ridiculous as a first essay at punting. A boat, when being towed, should not be allowed to get far out in the stream; keep her nose only slightly away from the bank you are skirting. Towers may be recommended not to gambol at the end of the line, and not to upset fishermen. The Thames angler is a patient creature, and deserves to be kindly treated.

Punting is out of the question for a long journey, and

requires not only a good deal of practice, but also local knowledge of currents and the river bottom. Once, however, you can keep a punt straight, and know your ground, there is nothing like it for sheer luxury. As a rule, in a punt two are company and three are none.

For a final word, you may be recommended before stepping into your boat to assure yourself, however respectable your boatman, that the most handy instrument for dealing with locks—viz., a compound boat-hook and paddle —has not been omitted, and that you have not been supplied with a cranky old pair of sculls, worn through at the leather and worn away at the button. Such things do happen.

Boating is, on the whole, an inexpensive amusement. You should get a boat almost anywhere, for practically the whole day, for 1s. 6d. a head—unless, of course, you do not return to your starting-place, but leave the boat to be called for. The following table gives in a handy form the prices charged for excursions down the river from Oxford:

	Teddington. £ s. d.	Eton. £ s. d.	Henley. £ s. d.	Extra Hire. Day. Week.
Canoe, Whiff, Outrigged Dingey (for one person)	1 10 0	1 5 0	1 0 0	2 0 10/-
Dingey, Sculling Gig or Skiff, Double Canoe	2 0 0	1 15 0	1 10 0	3 - 15/-
Pair-oared Gig, Canadian Canoe	2 10 0	2 5 0	2 0 0	
Randan Gig, Thames Skiff	3 0 0	2 15 0	2 10 0	5 - 20 -
Four-oared Gig, Randan Skiff	3 10 0	3 0 0	2 15 0	
Eight-oar	5 0 0	4 10 0	4 0 0	7 0 30/-
LARGER BOATS:—				
Large Shallop Four-oar	6 0 0	5 0 0	4 0 0	7 6 30/-
Large Four-oared Gig, with side seats Randan Pleasure Skiff	4 0 0	3 15 0	3 10 0	
Pair-oared do. 10ft. to 20ft., with side seats	3 10 0	3 0 0	2 15 0	5 - 20 -
Do. do. 16ft. to 18ft.,	3 0 0	2 15 0	2 10 0	
Ditto, fitted with tent cover and mattress	3 15 0	3 10 0	3 5 0	7 6 30 -
Randan, do. do.	5 0 0	4 10 0	4 0 0	

These prices include hire of boat for one week, after which extra hire is charged. It should be added that when a boat is left to be called for, a fee of 2s. 6d. is usually charged at the receiving boat-yard.

CAMPING.

CAMPING out on the Thames cannot be honestly recommended for any one with a greater sense of responsibility than the average undergraduate. You may, of course, sleep under canvas without catching cold, if you are lucky enough to hit on a dry summer; but no doubt the authors of this book exercised a sound discretion when they abandoned their arrangement of hoops and awnings to throw themselves into the arms of the riverside inn-keepers — harpies less rapacious, perhaps, except at Maidenhead, than they are described to be. Still, for those who are free from that sobering sense, there are few more enjoyable outings than a week or ten days' camping on the river. What freedom from restraint, when every man is for the nonce his own cook, kitchen-maid, bed-maker, and valet! What opportunities for the study of natural history! The habits and tastes of the water-rat

and other fearful game are no longer a secret to you. And the thing is delightfully easy to contrive. Salter, of Oxford, and most of the larger boatmen down-river, will supply you at short notice with every requisite, down to a neatly-packed hamper of crockery. You may either have a boat equipped with waterproof awning (*vide* the description of the *Rover*, in chapter i.), or you may take a tent. The tent is better fun on the whole.

As for camping-places, they are easily found, though the old days of camping at one's own sweet will on any private lawn have gone. The simplest plan is to ask a lock-keeper where you may pitch your tent. He will often be found to have an eligible island at hand ; he will, at any rate, direct you to a field where you may take up your quarters. A shilling a night is often charged for such accommodation —not very extortionate perhaps. The lock-keeper, by-the-way, will give you eggs, milk, and butter of a morning, or tell you where to get them.

The following is a list of camping-places which have been actually used, though inquiries must still be made before pitching, as owners and lock-keepers change :— Below Ifiley Lock ; at Rose Island; above Sandford Lock; below Abingdon ; above Day's Lock ; at Moulsford (leave obtained from the " Beetle and Wedge ") ; at Tilehurst ; on the island above the bridge at Henley ; above Spade Oak Ferry, near Bourne End ; and below the island at Penton Hook. Goring and Mapledurham are, or recently were, awkward places for camping purposes.

Things are a little less civilized above than below Oxford; but if a party has energy to go camping at all, they will probably have a more entertaining time—certainly a more exciting one—between Lechlade and Oxford than between Oxford and Teddington. It may be added, in case the tent should be found to leak, that there are one or two snug inns above Oxford absurdly reasonable in their charges.

EXCURSIONS.

WERE it not for the attractions of Richmond there would be comparatively little pleasure-boating below Teddington Lock. The tide introduces an unpleasant element in the difficulties of watermanship, and the banks of mud and gravel at low water offend both eyes and nose. And yet it is not so long ago that a person thought it natural enough to step into a boat at Chelsea for an afternoon or evening paddle. If the proposed lock below Richmond be ever built, the crowd of boats between Richmond and Teddington will throw Molesey and Maidenhead deep into the shade.

Of the river above locks, and within easy reach of a day from London, there may be said to be three zones— the first, distinctly suburban, extending from Teddington through Kingston, Hampton, and Chertsey to Staines; the second, from Staines through Windsor, Maidenhead, Marlow, and Henley to Sonning ; and the third, from Sonning to Streatley. The favourite beverage among excursionists in the first zone appears to be bottled beer ; in the second, particularly above and below Maidenhead, champagne bottles may be observed floating in the stream ; in the third, honest stone jars of cider or shandygaff are felt to be more in accord with the landscape.

On Saturday and Sunday afternoons the crowd is likely to be terrific in the first zone. Unless, therefore, the crowd itself be the object of your curiosity, you are not recommended to select this zone for your operations. The fun at Molesey Lock, a scene possibly busier, and certainly noisier, than Boulter's, may be observed with greater comfort from the towing-path than from the river. That these suburban reaches should be crowded is natural enough, but the reasons why the third zone is select as compared with the second are three : *First*, whereas the second zone is served both by the Great Western from

Paddington and by the South-Western from Waterloo, the third zone can only be reached by the Great Western. *Second*, the railway journey in the latter case takes from fifteen to twenty minutes longer. *Third*, the Great Western gives you cheap excursion tickets to Windsor, Maidenhead, Cookham, Marlow, and Henley, but no further. So powerful are these reasons, that but for the existence of Reading Streatley, Pangbourne, and Mapledurham would be as free from day-trippers as Wallingford. And yet the train service between Paddington and Reading is excellent, and between Paddington and Goring very fair.

Here let intending visitors be recommended to take their lunch with them in a hamper if they are starting for the whole day. Supper in some riverside inn at the end of a long journey accords well with the fitness of things, but as for lunches at such inns—well, time, temper, and digestion are saved by avoiding them. The rooms are often crammed, cold beef and mustard pickles seem to exhaust the bill of fare, and a good salad, the vision of all others conjured up by the landscape, remains a dream. But if you do go picnicking, sink or bury your empty bottles and refuse.

It may be useful to give the novice two actual instances of excursions comfortably to be made within a single day from town.

MARLOW TO WINDSOR.

PERHAPS the best journey for the purposes of mere sightseeing is that from Marlow to Windsor. This is a good but not severe day's work, and the mere mention of the places passed on the itinerary will show its interest. You catch an early train at Paddington for Marlow, making sure of getting there not later than eleven. Arrived at Marlow, you have a stroll of some ten minutes to the bridge, above and below which lies a whole flotilla. Once afloat, paddle or tow up-stream for half a mile or so in order to get a glimpse of Bisham Abbey. Then turn, and after passing the weir you will see the lock on your right. You have next a glorious view of the Quarry Woods as you swing past them, and, after a stretch of flat and somewhat bare meadow-land, you reach Bourne End, and then, a mile further on, Cookham. Here you should take a stroll through the churchyard, and then make your way down the straight cutting which leads to the lock. Cookham Lock is one of the gems of the river. Not only is it embowered in foliage of its own, but it has the whole range of the Cliefden Woods for a backing. When a Thames lock is set up on the London stage, the first the scene-painter selects is pretty sure to be Cookham. It is impossible to see too much of the Cliefden Woods, and so, when you have got through the lock, turn up to your left and visit the weir. Here it may parenthetically be remarked that it is as much safer to visit a weir from below than from above as it is easier to fall in than to get out of the water. Don't run into it, that is all. However, when you have got under weigh, drop down-stream for half a mile or so, and turn up the back-water to the right. This particular back-water is pretty enough in itself, but is especially worth a visit for the magnificent view it affords of the Cliefden Woods and of the house itself, seen in perspective between two arching elms. If you are wise, you will have brought your lunch, and will eat it here. Lunch over, you traverse the graceful sweep of Cliefden Reach and come to Boulter's Lock. As you will have read earlier in these pages, this is on Sunday afternoons a remarkable sight. From the variety and the quantity of its traffic it may be called the Piccadilly Circus of the Upper Thames. When through the lock, or over the rollers, it is well here, as at Cookham, to turn up to your left and visit the weir—the back-water leading up to it is so good. Boulter's Lock, through Maidenhead to Bray, is the next stage. At Bray you should visit the Church and the Almshouses, and then make your way to the lock. A long stretch of three miles takes you past Monkey Island and Surly to Boveney Lock. After passing this, Windsor Castle dominates the landscape as the Eiffel Tower does Paris, and the full view of it bursting upon you as you emerge from the shadow of the railway-bridge is majestic enough to crown any day of sight-seeing.

From Windsor you can drop down to Romney Lock, following the tow-path where the stream divides, and, without passing through the lock, land for a glimpse of Eton and the Playing-fields; or you may pass through the lock, turn up the back-water, and land any of your party who care for it to stroll through Eton to the inn at Windsor where you have elected to sup. The boat you must take back to the boat-yard where you have arranged to leave it. After supper you may have time before the last train goes to saunter up to the Castle, and to enjoy the famous view from its terrace.

STREATLEY TO CAVERSHAM.

FOR interest of a general kind the journey which has just been sketched is perhaps unrivalled, but there is another trip which for pure beauty of river scenery far surpasses it. The Thames from Streatley to Tilehurst is one uninterrupted stretch of loveliness passing before you like a pageant. There are no comparative wastes such as those between Marlow and Bourne End, between Maidenhead Bridge and Bray, to break the charm. The journey is not a long one; indeed, you can start from Streatley, row down to Tilehurst, and get back to Streatley in time for the last train, or you may go on to Sonning, or even Henley. Let us suppose that you are content with the single journey, and, preferring wisely to row with rather than against the stream, have, instead of getting out at Reading, decided to go on to Goring. A train leaving Paddington about nine will bring you to Goring before eleven. The walk from the station at Goring to the bridge which connects Goring with Streatley is a pretty one, and the vision of Streatley on the further side will probably make you reluctant to step at once into your boat. When, however, you do find yourself comfortably boated, you should first of all row up-stream as far as Cleeve Lock, one of the most wonderful half-miles to be found for river "bits." Then turn below the mill and make your way back to Goring Lock, and on past the glorious chalk hills of Streatley and the beech woods above Coombe Lodge to Pangbourne—a stretch of four miles or so. The lock, known as Whitchurch Lock, is here, as often elsewhere, the very focus of all that makes for picturesqueness, and you will probably be tempted to rest on your oars for some time, both above and below it, before you tackle the two miles which bring you to Mapledurham. The strong stream below the lock carries you all too swiftly over the short mile to Tilehurst. There you pass abruptly from enchanted ground into the prosy reach, redeemed only by long tangled hedges of brier-rose, which sweeps past Reading. At Caversham Bridge, about two miles from "The Roebuck" at Tilehurst, you leave your boat, stroll to Reading Station, and so back to town. The day's work is, as has been said, a short one, but such a scene as the Thames between Cleeve Lock and Tilehurst is not to be hurried through. If you take the journey at all, take it in sips, not at a gulp.

STEAMERS.

IN conclusion, but tell it only in Gath, the river can be seen from the decks of a couple of steamboats plying between Kingston and Oxford thrice a week!

Cassia Brothers, Printers, Chilworth and London.

www.ingramcontent.com/pod-product-compliance
Lightning Source LLC
Chambersburg PA
CBHW030300170426
43202CB00009B/817